Everything is Closed on Sunday

by Rin Stone

Everything is Closed on Sundays: Diaries of a Southern Queer Teenager

ISBN 978-1-949127-45-4

First Edition

Cover photos by Jeremy Gardels

Published by Deep Overstock, Portland, OR.

deepoverstock.com

DEEP OVERSTOCK
PUBLISHING

I don't really know what the goal of this is.

There's a lot of people who have done this before me, and who have done this after me, that I'm sure will write something incredibly meaningful.

Who have made their most intimate moments public.

Even though it's not needed, there's a part of me that wants to invite people to witness my viscera if they too are visceral, or if they're just curious.

In a way this is some kind of weird voluntary public disembowelment.

There are people like me, and there always have been.

This isn't special.

But, I want to make sure that everyone knows that.

Names have been changed unless permission has been given.

There are people in here who have since transitioned, and I am using their current pronouns even though I am misgendering myself in the past tense.

Part One: Center Point, Alabama

December 2nd, 2014

I don't feel as if I have to start on the 1st of January to start anew.

I have almost made it through the trainwreck that is 2014.

As you can see, I've already started my fruit sticker page.

I've been feeling happier the past few days because I've stopped giving the negative things so much attention. The negative things are still there, but I've either identified a solution and implemented it, or realized that there is no solution to the problem and moved on.

I'm going to be searching for a solution to my empathy sickness. I hope to write my progress.

I don't feel like complaining or being sad about things anymore.

Life is too short to live that way.

Does my life kind of suck a bit?

Yeah.

BUT, I can bear through this.

I can fix this.

My life will eventually not suck.

(It might suck again in a different period of suckitude, but there will be a point in which I will fully enjoy my life)

The suckitude I speak of is my first year of being a student at a Christian private school. I was coming to terms with my queerness and my place in spirituality, which from what we were being taught, was nowhere. I was also convinced that my mental illness for the most part was what I called "empathy sickness."

December 5th, 2014

I feel pretty today. It's silly for me to worry about my appearance so much, but I can't help it. I'm human and I want to feel like I'm attractive. I got my hair cut shorter yesterday and I love it. So many other people love it too.

I've gotten so many compliments

ANYWAY

I just wanted to write this because I hardly ever feel this way.

I want to try to write everyday, but so far I haven't been.

R is going to be moving in with mom and I.

I know mom and I might be judged, but this is the right decision.

People will say,

"It's sinful."

"She's underaged."

"It's temptation."

But, whatever.

Me, mom, and R can handle ourselves.

We'll clean the house and make it livable again.

This will be a new and short era of our lives, but we're all in this together.

R was my partner at the time. Her mother had kicked her out of the family home for smoking weed. Some religious folks in the south believe living together before marriage is sinful. The reaction people around us had to us being an interracial couple living together and before marriage was… less than kind.

December 10th, 2014

C and B spent the night last night.

I really like having friends over even though I also like to be alone. I need people and I hate it.

A lot of the reason for my sadness is mental and loneliness. I deny the fact that I need company in my head from others. I'd love to believe that I could bear this world alone.

But, I refuse to live a lie.

I really hope what I write in here isn't boring. I know I shouldn't care, but I wouldn't want someone to be bored of me if they were reading this.

What if I died?

What if I'm in a coma?

(By the way, if I am, try to communicate with my brain. Tell me to imagine pictures to see if I have brain activity. If you think I'll make it, don't pull the plug. R, Mom and dad reserve the rights to my life if I cannot choose.)

Didn't mean to get so morbid.

Oops.

It happens.

Anyway. I'm sitting in entrepreneurship class and eating cheese. That sounds weird.

I don't really like this class even though it's helpful sometimes.

I wonder if I'll ever open my own bookstore.

I wonder if I'll ever be published.

C and B were my only close highschool friends.

December 11th, 2014

Miss L used the word "clusterfuck."

I love that word.

She's mad at the school because it is in fact a clusterfuck.

Miss L was my history teacher at the time. She was the most human and the most kind teacher in the building. She didn't last long at this particular school, which makes sense because it was very cult-like, and she is very not cult-like.

December 15th, 2014

I never finished that entry. It was a busy day. R spent the night Saturday. This weekend was weird for me. I was super stressed and I had to take the ACT. I was gonna buy R's Christmas present this week. I love giving people stuff, but I'm broke. Someday, I'll have money to buy the people I love lots of stuff.

ANYWAY. I'm in a nice mood and I feel like writing.

Exams are tomorrow.

UGHHH. Noooo.

I'll just enjoy today for what it is.

I did very poorly on my ACT because a lot of the things we were being taught either weren't real, or were taught in a very bandaid slapping fashion.

Undated

"YOU'RE UNGRATEFUL"

okay

"I CAN'T HAVE A CAREER BECAUSE OF YOU"

okay

"YOU THINK YOU'RE AN ADULT AND HAVE SEX LIKE YOU'RE AN
ADULT, AND YOU'RE NOT"

okay

"I CAN'T STAND YOU."

okay

"I'M DONE WITH YOU."

okay

Door kicking

okay

Cabinets slamming

okay

Dishes clanking

okay

My mom and I had a very strained relationship at the time from being in close proximity since she and my dad got divorced. We were trauma bonded, and of course, had different experiences of this trauma. We are very close now.

December 17th, 2014

Mom and I fought again. Well, I kinda stood there while she yelled at me again. I won't go into too much detail, but she tried to kick my door in, and she compared me to my father by saying that I was manipu ing her even though she was the one manipulating me.

I'll be honest. I wanted to die. Sometimes I just want to die. I know she's depressed, but I cannot help her. That is her battle.

I know this shit sounds crazy, but sometimes I just want to see physical wounds in place of my mental wounds. I wanted to get drunk, but I didn't. It's exam week, and I can't be hungover.

I got my Beta Club pin and certificate, but mom probably won't care.

She never cares about the things I accomplish because she's focused on the bad.

"YOU NEVER WAKE UP ON TIME"

I have insomnia, agoraphobia, and panic disorder.

"I ALWAYS DO EVERYTHING FOR YOU."

I never ask her to.

December 23rd, 2014

Me, R, T, and M went to see Big Hero 6 two days ago, and I cried like a baby.

I like taking the kids places because they need to get away from their overbearing wayyyy too parenty parents.

I took some pictures of them for their mom as a Christmas present.

R's mom and stepdad will never accept my existence. Her stepdad thinks I'm a vagina with legs, and her mom thinks I'm only getting in R's way.

Why can't they just let me be important in her life?

I've never been this important to anyone.

I haven't been keeping up with my writing, but that's about to change.

T and M were R's little siblings. Her mom liked to find things to blame other than herself for why R was the way she was at the time, and a lot of times I happened to be that thing.

Undated

Last Wise Words of R in 2014

"Reverse shopping. It's when you take your stuff and put it on shelves in the store, then go home"

-R 2014

January 1st, 2015

So, today was okay.

R is sick and mom is home.

I kissed a semi-coherent R at midnight.

I started and ended another year with her.

She lives with me and mom now which is kinda fun.

It's like a slumber party that never ends.

We watched Parasyte and Fruit's Basket.

I'm not ready for school to start on the 6th.

ANYWAY

1st entry of 2015.

I become an adult this year.

I graduate this year.

I start college this year.

This year.

This year.

This year.

Undated

A list of things R shouldn't say.

1. "Toasty toasty fingers" ~

2. "Chicken bits"

3. "I'm snaking your boobs."

3 continued, "We can roleplay. I'll be the snake, and you can be the snake catcher."

January 6th, 2015

On Christianity

I used to think that I was a Christian.

Ever since I started private school, I don't think I am anymore.

I didn't know that there were so many Terms and Conditions.

I'm pansexual. I don't think God would hate me. I'm pro choice. I think women have power. I will not submit.

I have started to think about The Bible being a brain washing mechanism.

What if that's what it is?

I've never been to a church and felt welcome.

I've had more Christians bully me and talk down to me than queer people, atheists, etc. ever have.

I've had premarital sex.

I live with my girlfriend.

I do not believe I am a bad person.

Is there a God somewhere condemning me? Is there a God that is going to send me to Hell?

Did Jesus sacrifice for us? Is the universe God? Why was the proof of God's existence (The Bible) written so long ago, and why don't we have the first written proof if it's so important.

Are the things that I do Hell worthy?

Am I bad because I don't go to church?

Did Adam and Eve actually happen?

If I ask questions and admit my own faults and "sinful" actions to a "Christian" adult, I would be ridiculed and shamed for my actions and doubt against God and The Bible.

I AM LOST

January 9th, 2015

I don't feel like I'm alive.

I fled Mr. M's room.

My hand was so sweaty that I couldn't hold a pen.

I tried to feel normal, I really did.

I wish C would come here already.

I'm in the bathroom freaking out in a stall.

There's someone else in here.

They're really quiet.

My head is spinning. I wish this person would leave. LEAVE.

The lighting in M's room and the topic gives me panic attacks frequently.

My mom would make fun of me probably.

I hardly tell anyone about these things anymore.

Mr. M was the bible teacher.

January 12, 2015

I'm in Bible right now again. I'm feeling panicky again. It's so hot in here. My hands are getting sweaty again.

Yesterday R got paranoid with me. I'm not scared of her, I'm just scared of hurting her like that. I couldn't stop crying because I feel like I should be hurting if I hurt her.

She assured me that it wasn't my fault.

I still feel as if I'm awful.

She was crying and shaking.

Her eyes were full of fear.

I wanted to hug her, kiss her, and touch her; but I couldn't.

My arms feel weird. The lighting in this school trips me out.

We're fine again.

She's fine again.

I just wish I could disappear when I make her feel that way.

Every time I'm in Bible, I feel like I'm going to hell.

I hope I don't go to hell.

Is the Bible real?

No one can answer that for me.

Am I damned?

No one can answer that for me either.

Starting Revelations study today.

Help me.

R used various substances that unpredictably affected her mental state. Usually hallucinogens.

January 20, 2015

So, my bible teacher is saying that our culture is teaching that "tolerance" means that Christians can't say that homosexuality is wrong, or can't say that gays can't be involved in the ministry, or churches can't preform gay marriages. Well, I don't feel as if American Christians have the right to cry oppression. Christians have done nothing but oppress for a while in history. I'm not saying all Christians are bad at all, it's just that the modern Christian thinks they know what oppression is but they do not.

I thought I was a Christian until this school full of toxic ideas...

Reaped me of my voice

Took my individuality

Made me think I'm going to hell

They have oppressed me more than I could ever oppress them.

If I ever speak up, I will be yelled at or punished.

Yet, I'm still only mad at myself because I care too much.

What if we don't have souls?

Undated

Band names

Subtle Onions

No Bueno on Butt Sex

Disappointing Porn

January 22, 2015

Today has been rough. It all started when mom yelled about the kitten shitting on the floor when the dogs do it too. I ran out of gas. I was late to school. I almost got in a wreck. Mr. K told me I can't be a teacher's aid. I'm not taking no for an answer this time. I'm always easily let down or pushed away, but not this time. I will not be a pushover. Hot dogs for lunch. So much about this day that is wrong.

The principal let a student who was in an intimate relationship with a teacher, be a teacher's aid. I did not know he was in a relationship with her at the time, but found out shortly after we graduated and they got married. I wasn't ever allowed to be a teacher's aid to Miss L.

January 23, 2015

I had a dream that I had cancer last night. I was in a big hospital room. My body ached and my lungs were weak. There was a cannula and tank attached to me.

Everyone was crying.

I was about to die.

My dad was there.

I took a shower.

I crawled back in my bed after looking in the mirror. I was pale. My hair was short and smooth.

The nurse was crying.

Everyone told me that it was alright to let go.

They kept telling me that they loved me.

In the dream I was wondering if I would wake up somewhere else when I died.

Then I woke up.

I wonder if I had that dream because an angry part of me died last night. I wonder if a part of me died last night.

Did I die somewhere else last night?

Am I alive?

February 3, 2015

Too much has happened. Why am I surprised?

This is life. Shit happens.

R has been bad.

When she was drunk/on mushrooms I had to take care of her like I had to take care of dad.

The past two weeks…she's been crying a lot.

She got turned down from Jeff State and her financial aid because her GPA was so low.

She might go back to work for Vulcan.

I've been a huge mess too. I've thought about cutting. I want to starve myself, but I'm not. I'm eating. I'm living.

This school makes me miserable. I've been really sad. I want the best for mom, R, and myself, but there doesn't seem to be anything I can do for them but take care of myself for them. I have to be strong for them. They can't take care of me right now.

I always think I'm weak.

But I am not.

I am strong.

I am here.

I am breathing.

Breathing.

Breathing.

Vulcan is a steel mill in Alabama.

February 4, 2015

R told me to make fun of things in situations that hurt me. So, from now on I will make light of things again.

The preacher in chapel right now is very flamboyant and wearing khakis.

Anyone who willingly wears khakis is truly corrupted.

Today is alright though.

I just hate chapel.

For many reasons such as this.

ALSO CHRISTIAN ROCK.

Fuck Christian Rock.

If I have to hear

"How greeeaat….is our God!"

ONE. MORE. TIME.

I will explode.

March 3, 2015

Lots of time has passed since I last wrote.

Life has been weird.

My grades have gone down.

I turned 18.

I don't feel different.

I'm in Bible right now. I'm bored out of my fucking mind.

I don't belong here.

Enough about school.

R is trans or bigender.

She is still going by [he] and [x]

I 100% support and love her.

She's still figuring it out.

I'll write about this again when she's progressed.

I'm ready to start over.

No more sadness.

Blank slate. Clean pages.

I need to do this to write more.

I've been simplifying by donating clothes to the trans clothes exchange.

I only have 3 months of high school left. I'll be living with R on my own. I'll have a job. Childhood (Did I ever have one?) really would be over.

I feel dirty. I want to bathe. I want to dye my hair and wear my own clothes. I want to be in a sunny building or outdoors instead of this brick cell with no windows.

R came out to me as trans and I started learning what trans meant. I began to have a growing sense of doom in the coming years, knowing that I'd found what I am. I didn't speak of it until I was 20.

April 12, 2015

Hi.

It's been a while. I have a 48 pack of gel pens. So much has happened, so it'll take a couple of days to explain.

Friday (April 10) I did my first spoken word and it went great. I was the only young poet there. It's a poem called Older.

April 15, 2015

I was accepted to the Ada Long Writing Workshop.

Only 30 people are accepted.

I'm so excited.

For the next while I'll be writing about happenings from the past month or so that I haven't written.

STORYTIME

March 19, 2015. We went to the Aesop Rock and Rob Sonic (Hail Marry Mallon) show. It was amazing.

We left early because I panicked. I disappointed R even though she'd never say it.

Oh well.

We had a good time while it lasted.

Part Two: Homewood, Alabama

May 21, 2015

I graduated and R and I got kicked out by my moms landlord because she accused her of stealing.

ANYWAY.

Graduation was great.

Everyone was so proud.

It was everything I wanted it to be.

R and I are living on our own now. Dad is paying for most of everything.

He is being so great to me and R.

Mom is great. She's been my best friend for my entire life, but she needs to branch out. She needs to stop thinking about me for a while.

I feel bad that I haven't been writing much, but this year has been crazy.

I am finally free from what I hated for so long.

My mom's landlord was a family friend that didn't like the premarital interracial situation, and made up a reason to kick us out the second I turned 18, which was R stealing and pawning a power tool of some kind from their shed that was on the property, which she didn't do.

Undated

The man who claims that he is free to do as he pleases

But is a slave to his addiction

The woman who passes out money to her grandchildren

But waters down her soap

The mom who tells her daughter not to bite her nails

After her fifth drink at 3PM

The girl who wants to be a journalist

But can't breathe in the supermarket

Undated

I want to go home

July 17, 2015

This month has been strange.

Lots of tension between R and I.

I just left the house for the first time in 11 days.

We're waiting on the cable person.

My throat is itchy.

I feel too big.

I'm too curvy.

But, I'm still eating.

This was when my agoraphobia and psychotic symptoms began to peak.

August 11, 2015

I've done nothing but drag everyone down with me.

My agoraphobia is terrible.

I'm trying to get better.

I don't even know what to say besides, I'm ashamed.

I feel so empty.

I've made some new friends, but they're in CA, TX, and NY so…

I hope to meet them someday.

I love so many people but I'm so empty because I hate myself.

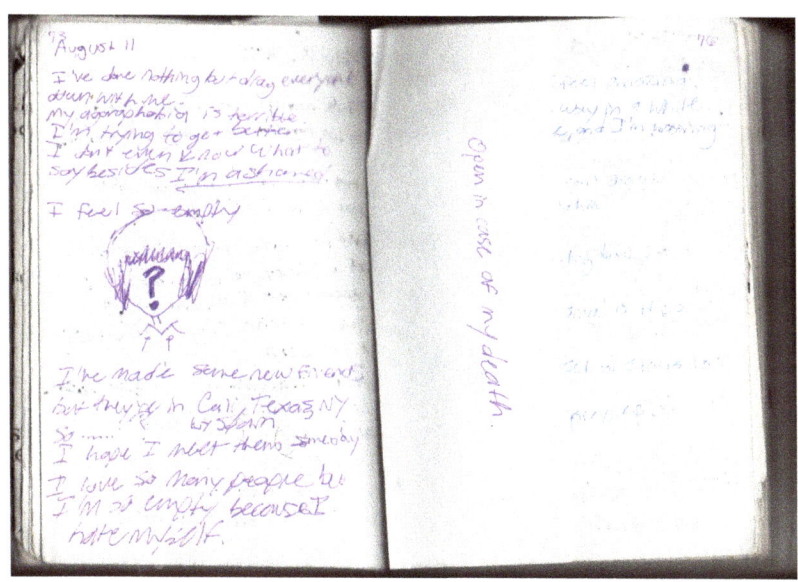

The only socialization I got outside of R and some other on and off partners was chat rooms on Tinychat.

Undated

[folded into the crease of the journal]

Open in case of my death

I want everyone I love to read my journals.

I want to make people happy.

I want to love people.

That's all I've ever wanted to do.

I want to write.

I want to save queer kids.

I WANT TO CURE MY SADNESS.

I'm full of it.

I was certain at this point that I'd die.

August 12, 2015

I drove today. I feel amazing.

I haven't felt this way in a while…

I've been outside and I'm wearing a cute outfit.

I'll be able to drive to the gas station soon.

I can't wait till school starts to be honest.

Life is about to pick up.

I hope.

?

I drove around the parking lot of our apartment complex.

August 18, 2015

4:49 AM

I thought I was great until other people told me I was undesirable when I was a kid.

I was short, stocky, tomboy.

I had the brain of a boy.

Everyone told me I was fat, bossy, loud, unladylike.

When I was 13 I lost 30lbs.

I softened my tone.

I said okay when that strange boy wanted to kiss me.

I said, "No I'm not" when I was told I was pretty.

Because if I said, "Yes I know" or, "Thank you" I was vain.

I missed running track with the boys, but now I had kissed all of them and my disorder didn't allow me to run freely.

Now, at 4:58 AM, I sit missing who I was.

If only at 13, I knew that at 18 I could love myself.

5:01 AM

_____

I knew I was a boy.

Only if at 13, I knew
that by 18, I could
love myself.

5:01 AM

9/20/2015

Be driven by joy

Not fear

I heard this from CGP Grey I believe.

9/21/2015

6:02 AM

I've never craved physical affection so much.

She never hugs me.

Holds my hand.

Sometimes that's what I need and she doesn't understand.

So she responds in fear.

I don't know what is my fault.

R had pure hatred and resentment for me at this point, for several reasons I'm sure.

9/22/15

I'm at my 2nd psychologist appointment. I'm so proud that I made it here.

October 3, 2015

Holly died on October 1st.

She shot herself in the head in R's grandmother's bathroom.

R's cousin's wedding is the last time I saw her alive.

We both already accepted her death a long time ago back in my 2014 journal when she tried to OD on Tylenol and we had to take her to the hospital.

Her ex is pretty shaken up.

I think he loved her.

[On October 5th, he told me he did.]

Rest in peace, Holly.

I'm sorry the world didn't treat you better.

Holly was R's aunt who we were very close with. Our relationship wasn't appropriate but it is what it is. There's more about her but those journals are gone, as they're either in R's family's storage shed, or a landfill. She was the casualty of the "you don't need mental healthcare when you have Jesus" mentality. It's okay to need Jesus AND mental healthcare.

October 6, 2015

I feel like I'm making a breakthrough.

I'm ready to live.

I've thought too much. I can't even write in this journal properly right now.

Sometimes I don't even feel real.

There's so much going on that I haven't written, so I will make up for that now.

→ So just now, a wasp almost landed on me. I ran inside and ripped my pants off because I thought that it went up my pants.

First things first.

We're thinking about moving to Portland, Oregon.

WHY?

So it sorta turns out that dad is still a huge dick sometimes.

My agoraphobia has gotten so bad that I have to take online classes and he's mad about that.

So mad in fact, that he pitched a drunken fit in the airport and decided that he'd take my car and home that he paid for with my child support.

His wife (W) says that he thinks it will make me better and that I should go back to mom's

W said he just wants what's best for me. R told me that I wasn't going to take the car back. Dad said I could have the car back when I'm "well enough to drive".

W said that I would come around and that I'm having a teenage tantrum.

Except I'm not. I will not take the car back.

Dad's punishing me for being mentally ill and that's REALLY not okay considering he caused most of my issues.

He's spent all of my child support paying for my apartment that he's kicking me out of so now I don't even have child support.

I didn't think it through.

I should have taken it as a check.

The only help my dad has offered me mentally is Valium that he bought from someone in Mexico.

ALSO →

My mom is drowning in her depression and is taking my dad's side just so she doesn't have to deal with his shit.

That's okay, but she can't expect me to stick around if I'm only getting worse because of her and dad sucking at being parents right now.

→ I'm grateful for my life and that they raised me the best they could, but now it's my turn to make myself. My turn to parent myself.

SO THAT'S WHY

My dad and I have not spoken in 3 years.

Undated

Dear dad,

I'm grateful for everything you've done for me. You have made a lot possible for me. But now, I'm going to go do for myself. The difference between me and everyone else is that I don't care about how much money you have. I don't care about material possessions. I am grateful for what I have received, but not attached. This is why you can keep my car. I don't want it. You taking it now means that you will use it to get points across to me. So, thank you for letting me use it, but I don't want it.

I understand why you're kicking me out. You're your own person with your own life and you can't be dealing with this mess, but I won't go back to mom's. I will not be cornered in a shitty house in Center Point. Mom will not make me better. Neither of you understand my mental illnesses, and that's fine. But, that means I know more about what would make me better, and living with my mom in Center Point will not make me better.

So, this is me being independent. You and mom never really gave me the chance to be until now, and the second it doesn't go perfectly, you both bailed. I will make something for myself. My illnesses will not stop me. I'm not mad at you, I never really have been. This year, I found out that no one knows what they're doing. We're all just trying to figure ourselves out. I love it and hate it all at once.

Thank you for everything you've done for me.

I know you're not perfect,

But I'm not either.

-Katie

[December 5, 2015

UPDATE

→ I never sent it to dad because he disowned me.

"Bye. Good riddance you ungrateful child."

Even when he is dying,

I won't forget these words.]

10/10/2015

One year ago today, my cousins and I were at dinner with my dad.

One year ago today I didn't know that dad would be my worst enemy.

I thought we were okay.

One year ago today I could not decide for myself.

One year ago today I thought my parents cared.

One year ago today I wasn't this bad.

One year ago today I didn't hate myself.

One year ago today.

One. Year. Ago. Today.

December 5, 2015

I've had this journal for just over a year.

So much has changed.

R and I have been at her mom's since the 1st, and let me say we are not at all very welcome here.

We kinda broke in though.

So what can I really say?

While sorting our stuff to put in a storage shed, I was thinking.

If M taught me one thing, what would that be?

THE ANSWER

"Don't take yourself too seriously."

Take yourself and everything around you as it is and move on.

Pages ago I wrote,

"I'm finally free from what I hated for so long."

BUT. What I hated goes so much farther than high school.

I hated every aspect of my life.

M is Holly's partner with whom I had an unusual and inappropriate relationship with. He was a man in his 40's.

December 6, 2015

My writing is shit because we're on the highway.

I'm freaking the fuck out to be honest.

I just wanna be out of this car.

Ugh.

I had some sort of PTSD meltdown at the apartments.

I was mad at R for no reason and I broke a garbage can.

I never thought panic attacks could be like this.

I just fake it till I make it.

December 11, 2015

We're staying at T's house.

His mom and sister are very very nice.

His mom lets us have sandwiches.

While I was making some tea she offered me honey, and S gave us mac n cheese.

During all of December of being homeless, R cried over her cacti 5+ times.

#1 started when she was at the door with them after falling asleep at the wheel and crashing into a guard rail, dumping out the cacti.

M called me tough.

No one has ever called me that before.

R and S were smoking in here with the door closed, and I accidentally got a bit high.

I have a respiratory infection.

It really sucks.

I think S is really pretty. She crosses her legs and toes. She touches her face a lot and tucks her hair behind her ears. She wears comfortable clothing that most people wouldn't find attractive but she's so…

Attractive.

She doesn't give a shit.

I love it.

T and S are friends of R's, and were involved in dealing drugs and such. Nice people, though.

December 20, 2015

The day I stopped giving a fuck.

First things first.

→ I'm on an airplane.

Willingly.

Thanks to Klonopin.

I feel so goddamn good.

I started taking Klonopin yesterday.

It makes me feel so normal.

I don't dissociate.

I see everything.

BUT

Quite frankly at the moment,

I'm a bit fucked up.

R gave me Klonopin to be able to go from not being able to be outside, to being able to be on an airplane. It worked, and I'm grateful, but I also became addicted to benzos.

Part Three: Portland, Oregon

December 23, 2015

I walked three blocks today to Cafe Eleven with R and we ordered Earl Grey, Silver Tipped Jasmine, and cookies.

I left them a cute note.

My brother tried to take me to the social security office and I had a meltdown.

I held his hand back to the car.

He told me I'm not a failure.

I'm not a failure.

My parents withheld my social security card, birth certificate, and bank account. You're legally a minor until 19 in Alabama.

January 3, 2015

Waking up to freezing pixels is a wonderful way to start my blank slate.

A sheet of white blankets all of what I knew.

I must create my world now with mental coding.

I feel the erasure of past anchors.

I can only hope I'll let them sink alone.

Undated

All along it was my fault that I'm alone.

Undated

I promise that you're never alone.

You feel alone because you aren't yourself right now.

But I'm still here.

You're still here.

You made it.

You have a job.

You're in Portland.

You're alive.

You're alive.

You're alive.

Undated

Hey Katie,

It's me,

You.

I know that I've been neglecting you and your good nature lately.

I know this because I was mean to R, and she left me in this room and said,

"I'm not taking this."

My first instinct was to lay on the floor with you, this journal.

Whenever I'm in doubt about who I am or how I feel, I refer to you.

I see who I was, and still am.

Who you are.

Who you are in here, is a lot better than who I am out there.

I just wanted to apologize to you.

I'm sorry.

I'm the version of you that's angry, mean, upset, and

Incredibly

Terribly

Broken.

You never let your past or angry feelings take hold of you, and I'm sorry I'm letting it take hold of you now.

I felt like I was back to being you while I was curled up on the floor with the journal, thinking of how much I changed.

I promise that I will fix this.

February 26, 2016

How long will I be disappointed in myself?

2016

I feel bad for not writing for so long. I've been taking a break I guess.

UPDATE

I work at Taco Bell, and I made a friend.

Her name is J.

ANYWAY

I had a weird ass dream where I was smoking weed with my high school art teacher on a front porch in a comfy chair while he drew a spicy picture of a woman with vitiligo.

June 30, 2016

I haven't written in here much this year at all.

It's kind of sad.

My creativity is dying, and my brain is overloaded with shit because of it.

I started a job, as I've said before.

It wears me out.

(A dog just said hi to me omg I love dogs ugh.)

Anyway, I have to do something about my creative overload, and fast.

I'm starting to have scary delusions.

One of them was, I was seeing dad for the first time in ages.

I was pregnant, and he shot me in the belly.

, hard to write ahhhh

There's a girl next to me wearing a cookie cat shirt.

Why do people talk on the phone on public transit?

Why do they do this?

Why are they like this?

OH GOD HE'S MAKING A THIRD PHONE CALL. UGH.

11/09/2016

I've noticed that the more depressed I am, the less I write in here.

It's been pretty bad.

Sometimes I feel like I have so many feelings that my only coping mechanism, writing, won't work.

I'm fighting the unknown and it's hard.

I might write some feelings later.

It's all too much right now.

01/11/2017

P and I went ice skating and decided that we'll go out and do stuff more.

Rock climbing is next.

After, we went to Denny's with R.

It started snowing!

We had an awesome diner moment, and decided to go to P's house.

On the way I had a meltdown and thought the day might be ruined, BUT, P gave me her gloves, and R helped me pull up my hood.

I felt so loved.

We made it to P's neighborhood and went to an antique shop.

R and I got some shirts, and R found a drawing of a unicorn with "badass bitch" over the top of it. It was framed and only $6, so we got it.

So, we went to P's and we drank champagne while petting cats and playing cards against humanity.

Much to our amazement it had started to snow hard, so we decided to head home.

P walked us out of her neighborhood in the most magical walk of our lives.

The snow was thick, there were snowmen and people on skis.

P and I had a tiny snowball fight.

All I could say is "This is amazing!"

"Amazing!"

"Wow!"

We made it to the train stop, hugged, and got on the train in a polar express-vibe moment.

It took R and I three hours to get home, but we witnessed people being social and kind in a city where people can be standoffish.

When we got home we ate pizza and fell asleep.

This was the best and most magical day I've experienced so far here in Portland.

I'm so thankful for this little blip of existence that I have

---

P was the first friend I made after moving to Portland. She ended up staying R's friend and not mine.

5/6/2017

I feel guilty for never writing in my journal anymore.

It's as if my life has just swallowed me and changed the very foundation of things I care about.

Now, I draw more than I write. I used to never see myself being any good at drawing, but that's because I never tried.

I have my dream job now that I wanted ever since I could legally have a job.

I work at a coffee shop.

It's been amazing.

I can't believe I live on the West Coast.

I also started Celexa and Ativan.

It's helped my anxiety A LOT.

Things are looking up.

Maybe this pencil will see more pages soon.

I had dared not dream bigger than the coffee industry. I did not know what I was allowed to want or dream of.

8/30/2017

I finally made it to the Japanese Garden.

I went with my brother and it was awesome.

I love being able to go outside and love my life.

There's still a lot of progress I can make, but I'm so happy I'm able to do some things.

9/29/2017

1:42 AM

I had an amazing day with my girlfriend.

I've come so far since this time last year.

Today we went to a tea shop, magic shop, and book shop.

I've never been able to do so much without having a panic attack.

At the magic shop, I bought a carnelian in the shape of a heart.

The lady at the counter asked if it had any meaning to me because it has a hold in the middle as if it's been shot.

It does. I'm too nervous to trust and love and be and take charge because of my PTSD, or rather, as a result of it. I didn't say this though.

I said, "I guess. Since it's the first one I noticed."

Also, while I'm here.

I've been promoted to barista and we also have to move out of our house by February because our landlords/roommates need their room back because they have a growing family.

This is the most amazing family I have ever had the pleasure to witness and I'm so happy that they've been so gracious and kind.

I wouldn't take all of these hard years back for anything.

I need to carry this journal with me more but sometimes I just want to get a new journal because carrying around this Struggle Tome feels burdensome sometimes.

I intend on completing this one though.

I guess that's all that I have to say for now.

I am finally some kind of happy and have some level of inner peace.

I think that this has come with learning how to trust myself and not to take myself too seriously.

What other people think of my neurodiversity is their problem, not mine.

Thank you for being here patiently waiting for me to write in you.

I love you.

10/16/2016

I had a dream about a coworker.

He was wearing lots of bracelets and rings.

We were on the phone but I kept going back and forth from being me and being him.

I could see from his point of view.

He had bandages all over from self harm.

He had tried to kill himself.

It was fucking weird.

Undated

Things That Have Fucked Me Up

- My dad

- My aunt telling me that I lied about my mental illnesses.

- Grandmother going to my school and telling them that I'm faking panic attacks.

- Passing out randomly and frequently as a result.

- Not being taught how to live and having everything ripped away from me.

- Self harm.

- I thought the people I have sex with liked me as a person.

- Work firing me because they thought I was "slow"

- R dealing out of our Alabama apartment.

- Her selling DXM to some kid who almost died on my floor as a result. I had to make him drink activated charcoal. She wasn't there for that.

- One of the people she sold to broke into our apartment when I was the only one home.

- One night during a panic attack she said the meanest things to me. That she wanted me to feel like I'd ruined her life and that she hopes I suffer. I think she was on something. I don't know what.

- Her addiction problem in general.

- My meltdowns.

- My eating disorder.

- The car wreck.

- Alabama.

- Christian School

- -I thought I was going to hell.

- -I was always drunk

- I'm in pain all the time.

- PTSD.

- ASD.

- Watching my cousins become more successful than me.

- Never having a secure place to live.

- Dad almost shooting me.

- Me giving my dad the keys when he told me he'd drive himself into the lake.

- Dad playing sad Eagles songs over and over and over and over and over and over and over and over on school nights or literally any other time.

- Dad building automatic weapons in the basement.

- Dad disowning me.

- Dad leaving me for someone else.

- I don't want to be a girl. I don't want boobs.

- Everyone telling me to forgive dad.

- My parent's hypochondria.

I'll continue later.

Or maybe not.

I wanna change.

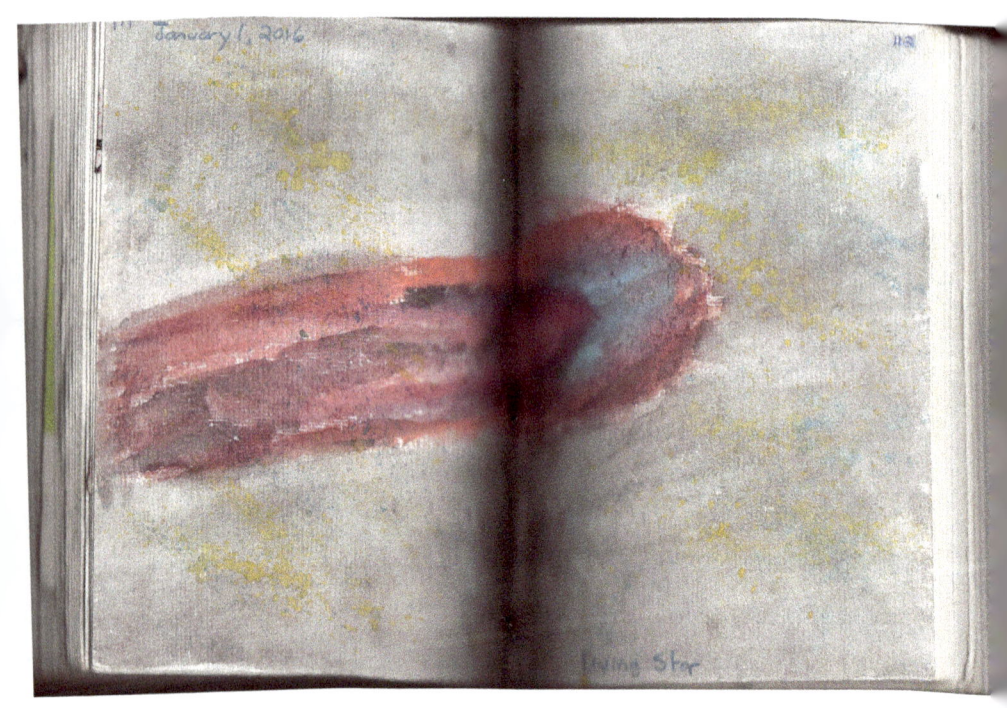

Undated

Another Mother Tongue

Judy Grahn

SM gave me this to read.

I love him.

He's lovely.

Apparently purple is a gay color and there's a lot of purple stuff in mythology.

SM was the first other trans man I ever met. I perceived him as my best friend, and I loved him very much. He did not feel this way about me. I was too clingy, and we are no longer in contact. It's one of my biggest regrets.

March 8, 2018

My brother just left.

I smoked a blunt and now I'm calling counseling services because I'm unwell.

My friend SM gave me resources and it's kinda pushing me to.

I appreciate it.

He won't be friends with me unless I actively try to get better.

I love him and Jordan so I have to get better.

For them and for me.

Mostly for me.

But, I won't lie and say it isn't because of them.

I love them.

I feel like my brother died even though he didn't.

I just know I may never see him again.

That sounds exaggerated, but that's how I feel.

He saved my life.

Or.

Helped me save my life.

Without his help I'd be dead, or worse, living with my parents feeding me their traumas and insecurities to a point where I feel like they're my responsibility.

I'm a different person.

I'm a person.

Before Portland I didn't feel like a person.

I had no clue who I was or what I liked or what I wanted.

I'm so grateful

For this little

Blip of existence

I share with

The people I love

Jordan is currently my partner.

May 5, 2018

I'm ending this journal.

I know there are several blank pages left, but I can't carry the weight of this journal anymore.

R and I broke up.

I was being used.

She wasn't getting better, so I moved out.

We got together when I was 15, and so much has changed.

I'm a different person.

I can't spend my time taking care of people that don't even care to get better.

So, that being said,

FUTURE ME,

Don't let your kindness be taken for granted.

Don't let people make you feel so worthless and helpless.

You are worth so much more.

You are your own person.

Be your own parent.

See what you want.

Take it.

I love you.

So many other people do too.

Thank you for the outlet these past three years.

Rin Stone

21 yrs

5/5/2018

Thank you for the
utlet these past
three years.

Over & out

Rin Stone
21 yrs
05/05/2018

Afterword

This book was written using entries from my journals I kept as a teenager until the age of twenty-one. I've been writing since I knew how to hold a crayon, and most of this writing has been a personal catalog until now. My first works consisted of tales about birds, and my dog's farts. Anyway, I want to share this part of myself, the most *cringe* part of myself, the *teenage* part of myself, in hopes someone else sees themselves reflected in these experiences.

These writings are in no means a moral compass if you couldn't already tell. There are many things past me and current me disagree on. I've omitted especially egregious and gratuitously morbid entries that I don't feel provide anything other than an audience to my teenage dumpster fire. Some things left in here toe that line, but that's okay.

Being a queer teen in the south is a unique experience that I'm sure varies depending on where you've ended up. Hell, being a teen, full stop, in the south is a unique experience. These writings aren't meant to demonize southerners, even though I was incredibly angry at my treatment by bodies of power in the region. There are good people in the south, and through these writings you've met one of them, and I hope you meet many more in your lifetime.

my soul today.

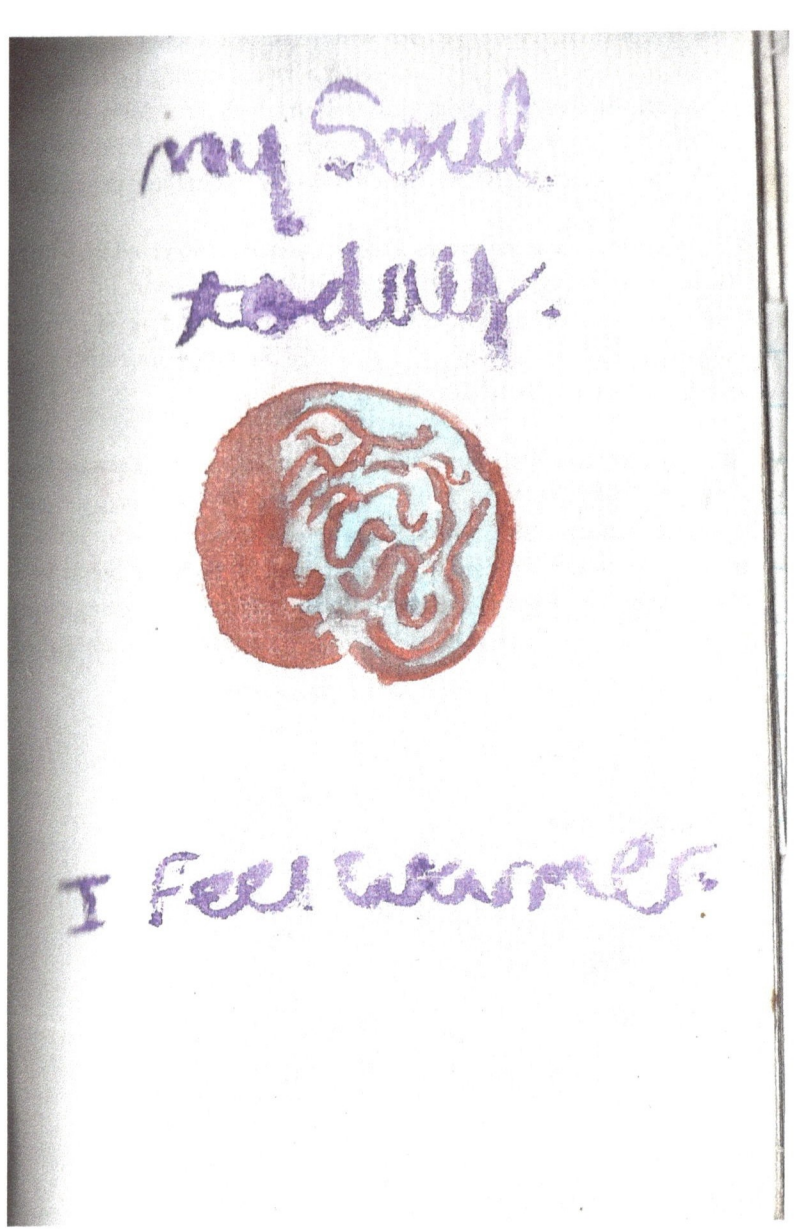

I feel warmer.

Author Photo: Jeremy Gardels, @aesthetic_shadows_photography

Rin is a North Alabama to Oregon transplant who has been writing ramblings since the age of four. He's been working in the book industry since 2018, and lives in Portland, Oregon with his partners and cats. He has an affinity for the unhinged, the queer, and the emotionally tumultuous. His current published works can be found in Deep Overstock Journals: DO#22: Knots and DO#21: Romance.

Milton Keynes UK
Ingram Content Group UK Ltd.
UKHW020849111124
451035UK00011B/885